salads &
side dishes

Also in the Chunky Cook Book series:

Vegetarian Main Dishes from around the world
Desserts & Drinks from around the world

salads &
side dishes
from around **the world**

Chunky Cook Books series
Salads & Side Dishes from around the world

First published in the UK in 2004 by
New Internationalist™ Publications Ltd
55 Rectory Road
Oxford OX4 1BW, UK.
www.newint.org
New Internationalist is a registered trade mark.

Cover image: © David Horwell

Food photography: Caroline Svensson, copyright © Kam & Co, Denmark
Email: studiet@kam.dk
Copyright © all other photographs: individual photographers/agencies.

Text copyright © Troth Wells/New Internationalist 2004 and individuals
contributing recipes.

Design by Alan Hughes/New Internationalist.

Printed in Italy by Amadeus.

Printed on recycled paper

British Library Cataloguing-in-Publication Data.
A catalogue record for this book is available from the British Library.

Library of Congress Cataloguing-in-Publication Data.
A catalogue for this book is available from the Library of Congress.

ISBN 1 904456 15 4

contents

PORTRAIT PHOTO CREDITS:
AMEDEO VERGANI – PAGES 8 & 140
CLAUDE SAUVAGEOT – PAGE 50
PETER STALKER/NEW INTERNATIONALIST – PAGE 110

introduction

Markets bursting with colorful fruit and fresh vegetables are often a high point of travel, whether in Spain or Canada, India or Mexico. Many of the once 'exotic' fruit and veg are now frequently seen in our local markets or supermarkets. Handy as this might be for us in the West, it may be at too high a price for the small producers. The fair trade movement works to guarantee that decent amounts reach the people who grow the food. In 2003, sales of fair trade goods reached over US$950 million and there were big increases in North America and Europe.

Fair trade is one burning issue (see page 170); organic food is another. More and more people want food that is not force-fed with fertilizer or poisoned with pesticides. In 2002, global sales of organic food and drink rose by over 10 per cent to $23 billion, according to the US publication *Organic Monitor*.

At first, Europe had the largest market for these goods but now North America leads. Organic production is booming, with almost 23 million hectares of organic farmland – much of it in the Majority World, where farmers are attracted to the export benefits of such food production.

More than 350 chemicals are approved as pesticides in rich countries. They kill insects, weeds and fungi, and protect crops from disease during their growth, transport and storage. The idea is that after industrial cleaning and washing at home, any harmful chemicals will have been removed before you pop that apple or carrot into your mouth. Wait a moment, though. Residual amounts can linger, as research by Britain's *Which?*

magazine has shown. Some of the worst-affected foods are apples, grapes, celery, pears, salmon, flour, peaches, lettuce and strawberries. But the good news is that many more that had been regularly monitored had no or low levels of pesticide residues: egg-plant/aubergines, sweet peppers, yogurt, eggs, cabbages, leeks, sea fish, goat's and ewe's milk, chicken and low-fat spreads.

Whatever you do, don't reduce your intake of fruit and vegetables. Opting for organic food means you do not have to worry about pesticide residues and you will be supporting many farmers in developing countries who want to break the link with agribusiness companies like Monsanto. Monsanto, pioneer of genetically modified (GM) seeds, also supplies many of the herbicides and knock-out chemicals to accompany them. The UN's International Trade Center expects 'confident growth expectations [for organics] based on a strong and increasing consumer awareness of health and environmental issues, including a growing resistance to GM food products.'

So look for the organic labels on bananas and produce from the global South. Shop at your local farmers' market; sign up for a box delivery of fresh healthy food. Or get digging yourself.

These recipes are easy to prepare and taste even better with fair trade organic goods. Have a look through and see the mouthwatering selection of side dishes and salads, many captured by the studio of award-winning Danish photographer Peter Kam. ∎

africa

sweet potato bread

serves **6**

½ pound / 225 g sweet
potatoes, cooked
and mashed

1 cup / 125 g
corn/maize flour

1 cup / 125 g wheat flour

2 teaspoons baking
powder

a little milk

salt

*Heat oven to
400°F/200°C/Gas 6*

1 Put the mashed sweet potato into a bowl and sieve in the flours, baking powder and salt. Mix everything together, adding enough milk to make a stiff mixture.

2 Now spoon the bread into a greased tin and cook for about 30 minutes. When it is ready, let it cool for a while and then serve it warm or cold.

spinach & peanut butter

serves **6**

2 pounds / 1 kg spinach, chopped

1 onion, chopped finely

2 tomatoes, sliced

1 green bell pepper, chopped finely

1 chili, chopped finely

4 tablespoons peanut butter

water

oil

salt

1 To begin, heat the oil in a heavy pan and sauté the onion until it is golden. Now stir in the tomatoes and bell pepper. Cook for 3 minutes before adding the spinach, chili and salt. Mix the ingredients well and then cover and cook gently.

2 While that is happening, put the peanut butter into a bowl and add enough warm water to make a smooth, flowing paste. Spoon or pour this into the pan and stir well.

3 Continue to simmer the spinach mixture, uncovered, for 10 minutes, stirring frequently to prevent catching. Add more water if you need to.

zucchini/ courgettes with peanuts

serves **4-6**

1$^1/_2$ pounds / 675 g zucchini/courgettes, sliced

1-2 cloves garlic, crushed

1 tablespoon lemon juice

2 tablespoons / 25 g margarine

1$^1/_2$ cups / 185 g peanuts, toasted and coarsely chopped

salt and pepper

1 To begin, simmer the zucchini/courgettes in very little boiling water for 5-10 minutes until they are tender. Drain well and put them into a bowl.

2 Now add the garlic, lemon juice, margarine, salt and pepper and mash all the ingredients with a fork. Add more lemon juice if required. Spoon the mash into a bowl and scatter the toasted hot peanuts on top before serving with millet or rice.

curried potatoes

serves **4-6**

- 2 pounds / 1 kg potatoes, diced and parboiled
- 1 onion, chopped finely
- 1 clove garlic, crushed
- $1/2$ teaspoon turmeric
- $1/4$ teaspoon chili powder
- $1/2$ teaspoon ground cinnamon
- $1/2$ teaspoon crushed cilantro/coriander seeds or ground coriander
- 1 teaspoon tomato paste
- 2 teaspoons lemon juice
- 1 tablespoon parsley, chopped
- a little water
- oil
- salt

1 Heat the oil in a pan and sauté the onion. When it is beginning to turn golden, add the garlic and cook for 30 seconds.

2 Now shake in the turmeric, chili powder, cinnamon and cilantro/coriander seeds and cook for about 1 minute to blend their flavors into the onion and garlic.

3 When this is done, mix in the tomato paste, lemon juice, parsley and salt. Stir before adding the parboiled potatoes. Stir the mixture well to distribute the sauce, add water to cover the base of the pan and then cook, covered, for 10 minutes or until the potatoes are tender and the liquid almost dried.

serves **6**

yataklete kilkil

potatoes with nutmeg

1 pound / 450 g new potatoes, diced

2-3 heads of broccoli

3 large carrots, sliced

6-8 cauliflower florets, chopped

2-3 tablespoons / 25-40 g margarine or ghee

1 onion, finely chopped

2 cloves garlic

1 teaspoon turmeric

1-2 teaspoons ground nutmeg

1 teaspoon ground cinnamon

1/2 inch / 1 cm fresh root ginger, peeled and finely chopped

1 clove

salt and pepper

1 First, steam or boil the potatoes, chopped broccoli stalks and the carrots for 10 minutes or so until nearly ready.

2 Then add the broccoli heads and cauliflower pieces and steam or boil together for another 4 minutes until all the vegetables are done. Drain.

3 Next heat the margarine or ghee and sauté the onion and garlic before adding the turmeric, nutmeg, cinnamon, ginger and clove. Then mix in the vegetables, season with pepper and salt and cook for 6-8 minutes, stirring frequently. Serve with millet or rice.

koocha 'fatty kunda'

serves **4**

spinach and peanut butter

1 pound / 450 g spinach, fresh or frozen, chopped

1 tablespoon peanut or other vegetable oil

2 medium onions, chopped finely

2 cloves garlic, crushed

12 black peppercorns, crushed

juice of 1 lemon

1 cup / 240 ml chicken stock

a few dashes of tabasco sauce, or $1/4$ teaspoon chili powder

1-2 tablespoons crunchy peanut butter

salt and pepper

1 Using a large pan, heat the oil and soften the onions in it. Add the garlic and peppercorns and cook for 3 minutes.

2 After this, put in the spinach, lemon juice, half the stock, chili powder or Tabasco sauce, salt and pepper and simmer gently for 8-10 minutes.

3 Stir the remaining stock into the peanut butter in a bowl and then add this to the cooking pot and mix it in well. Continue cooking for a further 10 minutes and then serve.

GHANA

tatali

serves **4**

plantain fritters

1 pound / 450 g very ripe plantains, mashed or liquidized

¹/₂ pound / 225 g corn/maize meal

1 onion, chopped finely

1 red chili, chopped finely

1 teaspoon ground ginger

1 egg, beaten

palm nut oil*

salt

*Available from Caribbean and Indian stores. Substitute peanut or other vegetable oil if you cannot find it.

1 Place the mashed plantains in a large bowl and shake in the corn/maize meal, mixing well.

2 Now put in the onion, chili, ginger and salt and combine all the ingredients. If necessary, add some beaten egg to help bind the mixture.

3 Divide the mixture into small patties, about 2 inches/5 cms in diameter and ¹/₂ inch/1 cm or so thick.

4 Taking a heavy pan, gently heat the palm nut oil. When it is hot place several of the fritters in it and cook for 5-8 minutes, turning once until they are crisp. Drain on kitchen paper and serve with curried black-eyed beans or pumpkin curry.

KENYA

rice &
spinach

serves **4-6**

1 pound / 450 g spinach,
fresh or frozen, chopped

3 tablespoons olive oil

1 onion, sliced

1 pound / 450 g rice

2$\frac{1}{2}$ cups / 590 ml
chicken stock

4 medium tomatoes,
chopped

1 tablespoon fresh
fennel, chopped or 1
teaspoon dried

1 medium tomato, sliced

1 hard-boiled egg, sliced

salt and pepper

1 Heat the oil in a large saucepan and cook the onion until it is soft and golden. Add the rice and fry for 1 minute.

2 Next put the chopped spinach in the pan and then the chicken stock.

3 After this, cover the pan and bring to the boil. Reduce the heat and cook gently until most of the liquid is absorbed, about 20 minutes.

4 Now add the 4 chopped tomatoes and fennel and carefully mix this in. Cover and cook again until all the moisture is absorbed and the rice is ready.

5 Season, and then decorate with the sliced tomato and egg slices.

sweet potatoes

serves **4**

with tomatoes

1 pound / 450 g sweet
potatoes, peeled

2-4 tablespoons / 25-50 g
margarine

$1/2$ teaspoon sugar

1 teaspoon chili powder

3 medium tomatoes,
sliced

salt and pepper

1 Boil the sweet potatoes, whole, in water until they are soft, about 30 minutes depending on the size of the vegetable. Drain and allow them to cool and then cut into $1/4$ inch/0.5 cm slices.

2 In a pan, melt the margarine and sauté the potato slices for about 5 minutes until golden brown. Add the chili powder, salt, pepper and sugar and mix well. Now put in the sliced tomatoes and cook for a further 5 minutes. Serve hot with grated cheese or cooked sliced sausage on top if desired.

MALAWI

boiled pumpkin

serves **4**

$^1/_2$ onion, sliced

2 scallions/spring onions, sliced+

1 pound / 450 g pumpkin, chopped

1 tablespoon parsley, chopped

a little water

$^1/_2$ teaspoon sugar+

2 tablespoons oil

salt and pepper

+optional ingredients

1 Heat the oil and sauté the onion followed by the scallions/spring onions if using.

2 When they are nicely softened, put in the pumpkin pieces and a little water barely to cover the base of the pan. Boil gently, with the lid on, for 10 minutes.

3 Then remove the cover and cook very slowly, stirring frequently so that the pumpkin does not catch, for 20 minutes or so, until it is cooked.

4 Season with salt and pepper and add a little sugar if liked. The dish can also be cooked in a low oven, uncovered for half an hour, after the initial 10-minute boiling period.

coconut rice serves **4-6**

¹/₂ pound / 225 g rice

1 onion, chopped

4 tomatoes, chopped

1 tablespoon tomato paste

¹/₂ teaspoon chili powder

2¹/₂ cups / 590 ml stock or water

1 tablespoon butter or margarine⁺

1 cup / 75 g desiccated coconut

1 cup / 240 ml coconut milk

salt

+ optional ingredient

1 First, bring the stock or water to the boil in a large pan. Put in the onion, tomatoes, tomato paste, chili powder and salt.

2 Reduce the heat, cover and simmer for 10 minutes before adding the rice and butter or margarine if using.

3 When the rice is in the pot, stir well and increase the heat to bring back to a vigorous boil. Then turn down to a more moderate simmer and cook for 20 minutes or until the rice is done and the stock has been absorbed.

4 Now shake in the desiccated coconut and mix into the rice. Pour in the coconut milk and combine all the ingredients thoroughly. Cook very gently for a further 5 minutes, stirring frequently.

SIERRA LEONE

frejon

serves **4**

beans with cocoa

1 cup / 225 g black-eyed
beans, cooked

$^1/_2$ cup / 120 ml coconut
milk

1 teaspoon ground mixed
spice

1-2 tablespoons cocoa
powder, mixed
to a paste with
a little water

1-2 tablespoons sugar

pinch of salt

1 Drain the cooked beans and put them into a bowl containing the coconut milk and sugar. Mix well and then partially mash them with a fork.

2 Now add the cocoa paste, the mixed spice and a pinch of salt; stir them in. Return all the ingredients to a saucepan and heat gently so that the flavors mingle before serving.

serves **4**

glazed sweet potatoes

1 teaspoon sugar or honey

1 tablespoon raisins or sultanas

$\frac{1}{2}$ teaspoon ground ginger

1 teaspoon cinnamon

juice of a lemon

grated rind of an orange

2 sweet potatoes, sliced and parboiled

a little water

2 tablespoons margarine

salt

1 Melt the margarine in a heavy pan and mix in the sugar or honey as well as the raisins or sultanas.

2 Next add the ginger, cinnamon, salt, lemon juice and orange rind. Mix well before pouring in a little water. Now put in the partially-cooked potato slices and stir them round to coat them in the sauce.

3 Cover the pan and let the potatoes cook very gently for 5-10 minutes, turning them from time to time so that they cook evenly and do not catch.

eggplant/ aubergine

with spices

1 pound / 450 g egg-plants/aubergines, cut into $1/2$ inch/ 1 cm slices

2 tablespoons sesame seeds

$1/4$-$1/2$ teaspoon powdered asafetida*

$1^1/_2$ teaspoons fresh ginger, grated

1 teaspoon paprika

$1/2$ green chili, chopped+

juice of $1/2$ lemon or lime

2 tablespoons fresh cilantro/coriander leaves, chopped

oil

salt and pepper

*Available from Indian food stores.

+optional ingredient

1 First place the egg-plant/aubergine slices in a colander and sprinkle them with salt to draw out the bitterness. Set aside for 15 minutes, then rinse and drain.

2 After this heat the oil in a large pan and when it is hot pop in the slices. Fry them quickly on both sides until they begin to soften (they will cook more later). Remove, drain on kitchen paper and set aside.

3 Using more oil if required, put the sesame seeds in the pan and add the asafetida, ginger, paprika, chili if using, salt and pepper. Stir briskly and cook for 30 seconds.

4 Now return the egg-plant/aubergine slices to the pan and stir in the lemon or lime juice. Mix all the ingredients well and then cover the pan and simmer on a low heat for 15 minutes. Sprinkle with the cilantro/coriander leaves before serving.

yellow rice

with raisins or sultanas

¹/₂ pound / 225 g rice

1 stick cinnamon

1 teaspoon turmeric

1 cup / 100 g raisins or sultanas

salt

1 Put the rice in a pan of boiling water and add the cinnamon stick, turmeric and salt. Boil vigorously for 10-15 minutes.

2 When the rice is almost cooked, stir in the raisins or sultanas, mix well and continue to cook for a further 5-10 minutes or until the rice is ready.

TANZANIA

carrot sambaro

serves **4**

spicy carrots

½ pound / 225 g carrots,
sliced finely and
parboiled

1 teaspoon mustard seed

½ teaspoon turmeric

1 clove garlic, chopped

½ green chili, cut finely

½ teaspoon sugar+

squeeze of lemon juice

oil

salt

+optional ingredient

1 Using a heavy pan, heat the oil and
put in the mustard seed and stir it
round for a few moments before
adding the turmeric, garlic and chili.
Cook together gently for 1 minute.

2 Now add the parboiled carrot slices
and stir them into the spice mixture
so they are coated. Add the salt and
sugar if using and mix. Cover the pan
and simmer slowly for 5 minutes.

3 Just before serving, splash the
carrots with the lemon or lime juice.

curried cabbage

serves **4**

¹/₂ pound / 225 g cabbage, chopped finely	**¹/₂ green chili, chopped finely**
1 onion	**1 tomato**
2 cloves garlic	**a little water**
1 teaspoon curry powder	**oil**
1 teaspoon mustard seed	**salt**
¹/₂ teaspoon fresh ginger, grated	

1 To begin, heat the oil and fry the onion gently until it is soft. Then put in the garlic, curry powder, mustard seed, ginger and chili.

2 Stir these ingredients together for 2 minutes over a gentle heat, to blend them.

3 When that is done, raise the heat, add the cabbage and fry for 3 minutes. Then put in the tomato.

4 Stir-fry these for 1 minute and then pour in a little water, cover, and cook over a low heat for 5 minutes or until the cabbage is cooked but still crunchy.

TANZANIA

futari

serves **6-8**

coconut milk pumpkin

2 cups / 300 g pumpkin, peeled and cut into 1 inch/ 2.5 cm chunks

1 pound / 450 g sweet potatoes, peeled and diced

1 onion, finely chopped

1 tablespoon oil

juice of $1/2$ lemon

2 cloves

$1/2$ cup / 50 g creamed coconut melted in 1 cup/ 240 ml hot water

1 teaspoon ground cinnamon

salt and pepper

1 In a heavy pan, cook the onion in the oil until it is golden. Then combine it with the pumpkin and sweet potato pieces.

2 Now add the lemon juice, cloves, salt and the coconut milk. Cover and simmer slowly for 10-15 minutes.

3 After this, add the cinnamon and seasoning. Cook, uncovered, for another 15-20 minutes until the vegetables are tender, stirring frequently to prevent sticking. Add more coconut milk or plain milk if the mixture becomes too dry.

TANZANIA

mint chutney serves 4

1/2 cup / 30 g fresh
mint leaves

1/2 cup / 30 g fresh
cilantro/
coriander leaves

handful cashew nuts

1 bell pepper

juice of 2 limes
or lemons

1 tablespoon sugar

3-4 cloves garlic

1-3 teaspoons cilantro/
coriander seeds

1/4 teaspoon chili
powder

water

1 Combine all the ingredients except the water in a blender, or chop them very finely and mix together. Add water as required and serve with meat dishes.

mkate wa ufute

serves **8-10**

pancakes

1 teaspoon dried yeast	$^2/_3$ cup / 150 ml milk
1 teaspoon sugar	3 tablespoons sesame seeds, toasted
$^2/_3$ cup / 150 ml warm water	oil
1 cup / 125 g flour	

1 Put the yeast and sugar into a bowl and pour on the warm water. Let it activate for 5-10 minutes until it becomes frothy.

2 Shake or sift the flour into a large bowl. Make a well in the center and pour in the yeast mixture, stirring as you do so.

3 After that, gradually add the milk, stirring continuously to make a thick batter.

4 Now heat a little oil in a frying pan. When it is very hot, spoon in some of the batter and spread it out into a circle, using the back of the spoon.

5 Let the pancake cook for 2 minutes on one side before turning over to brown the second side.

6 Sprinkle on the toasted sesame seeds for the final few minutes of cooking; then remove and keep hot while you cook the rest.

asia

AFGHANISTAN

egg-plant/ aubergine in yogurt

serves **4**

2 egg-plants/aubergines, diced	**$1/4$ teaspoon chili powder**
1 teaspoon ground coriander	**$1/2$ teaspoon garam masala**
1 teaspoon ground cumin	**oil**
$1/2$ teaspoon ground cinnamon	**salt**
$1/2$ onion, sliced finely	
$3/4$ cup / 150 g yogurt	

1 To begin, place the egg-plant/aubergine pieces in a bowl or colander, sprinkle on some salt to draw out the bitter taste, and leave them for 20 minutes. Then rinse and drain.

2 Heat the oil in a wok or pan and sizzle the coriander, cumin and cinnamon for 30 seconds before adding the onion.

3 Stir-fry that for a few minutes and then put in about half of the egg-plant/aubergine pieces.

4 When these begin to soften, remove them and stir-fry the rest, adding more oil as necessary.

5 The first batch of vegetables and spices can be replaced now; stir all the ingredients together. Cook until the egg-plant/aubergines are soft (about 5 minutes in a wok, up to 20 minutes in a saucepan).

6 When they are ready, turn down the heat and spoon in the yogurt, stirring well. Heat through without boiling and then serve, garnished with the chili powder and garam masala sprinkled on top.

miso potatoes

serves **2**

4 medium potatoes, cut into chip/french fry shape

1 tablespoon miso

1 tablespoon oil

2 tablespoons / 25 g melted margarine

Note: To reduce the cooking time, parboil the potatoes first for 5 minutes.

Heat oven to 350°F/180°C/Gas 4

1 Mix the miso with the melted margarine in a bowl.

2 Then spoon the oil into an oven-proof dish which has a tight-fitting lid and add the sliced potatoes.

3 Pour the miso-margarine mixture over the potatoes and stir round gently to distribute the sauce.

4 Cover and bake for about 20 minutes or until the potatoes are tender.

brindaboni

serves **4-6**

snowpeas/mangetout and sweet potatoes

1 teaspoon cumin seeds

1 teaspoon coriander
seeds

1 teaspoon turmeric

2 bayleaves

2 sweet potatoes,
thinly sliced

$1/2$ pound / 225 g
snowpeas/mangetout,
cut into 2 or 3 sections

oil

salt

1 First of all, toast the cumin and coriander seeds by heating them in a frying pan, without oil, shaking from time to time or moving them with a wooden spoon until they go a little brown. Then crush them in a mortar and set aside.

2 Now heat the oil in a heavy pan and add the turmeric, bayleaves and salt. Then put in the sweet potatoes and cook for 5 minutes, turning them frequently, until they begin to soften.

3 Add the cumin and coriander. Mix well.

4 Next pour in just enough water to cover the base of the pan and simmer, covered, for about 10 minutes or until the sweet potatoes are soft.

5 When they are almost ready, turn up the heat and put in the snowpeas/mangetout. Cook for 1-2 minutes and then serve.

BANGLADESH

saag

serves **4**

spinach

1 clove garlic, crushed

1 dried red chili *

**1 pound / 450 g spinach,
chopped**

1 green chili, chopped

oil

salt

* If the chili is not broken or
chopped, and therefore the seeds
are not released, then the chili will
not make the dish hot but will
impart a smoky flavor. Discard the
chili before serving if desired.

If you do not want a chili to be too
hot, then cut it longitudinally and
take out its seeds. The green or
red skin provides vitamin C
and also gives the dish a
pungent taste.

1 Heat the oil and then toss in the crushed garlic and the whole dried red chili and let them sizzle for a few minutes.

2 Now add the spinach and stir-fry for 3 minutes. After this, put the lid on and let the spinach cook in its own steam; do not add water.

3 Cook for 10 minutes and then add the green chili slices and seasoning. Serve with lemon wedges or mustard.

chutney rice serves 4

1 1/2 cups / 300 g rice

2-4 tablespoons sugar

4 tablespoons wine vinegar

3 cloves or 1/4 teaspoon ground cloves

2 large cooking apples, chopped

4 tablespoons raisins or sultanas

2 tablespoons oil

3 cups / 700 ml water

1/2 cup / 60 g unsalted cashew nuts

salt and pepper

1 Taking first the sugar, vinegar and salt, gently stir them together in a pan. Now add the cloves, apple and raisins or sultanas.

2 Next heat the mixture slowly, stirring frequently, and cook it for about 30 minutes or until it thickens. Allow to cool a little.

3 Meanwhile, gently heat the oil in a large saucepan. Add the rice and stir for about 1 minute, seasoning with salt and pepper. Then pour in the water, put the lid on, and bring to the boil. Now turn down the heat and simmer the rice for 20 minutes or until it is cooked as you like it.

4 When this is done, turn the rice into a dish and spoon the chutney over it, scattering the cashew nuts on top before serving.

cucumber & sesame seed salad

serves **4-6**

1 large cucumber

$^{1}/_{2}$ cup / 120 ml white wine or cider vinegar

1 tablespoon sesame seeds

1 tablespoon sesame oil

1 onion, sliced finely

2 cloves garlic, sliced finely

1 teaspoon turmeric

1-2 teaspoons sugar

salt

1 First peel the cucumber and cut into 2 inch/5 cm pieces. Cut these again into lengthwise sticks. Now put them into a pan with the vinegar and salt; add a little water to cover, heat and simmer for a few minutes until the cucumber is slightly tender and transparent. Drain, keeping the liquid, and let the cucumber cool. Set aside.

2 Now toast the sesame seeds in a pan with a little oil until they begin to jump and turn golden. Then let them cool.

3 After this, heat 1 tablespoon of the oil in a pan and cook the onion and garlic without burning until they are golden brown. Remove them from the pan and set aside.

4 Now pour in the remaining oil, turmeric, sugar and half the drained vinegar liquid. Stir this over a gentle heat until the sugar is dissolved. Add the onion and garlic and heat them through.

5 Arrange the cucumber pieces in a salad bowl and pour over the dressing. Mix well and then scatter the sesame seeds on top. Serve warm or cold.

chinese vegetables

serves **4-6**

4 scallions/spring onions, sliced

1/2 teaspoon fresh ginger, grated

1 red bell pepper, sliced

1 carrot, thinly sliced

1 cup / 110 g snowpeas/mangetout

1 stalk celery, cut into thin diagonal slices

1/3 cup / 80 ml water

1 tablespoon soy sauce

oil

salt

1 After the vegetables are prepared, heat the oil in a wok or large frying pan. When it is hot, put in the scallions/spring onions and ginger first and cook them for 1 minute, stirring all the time.

2 The bell pepper, carrot, snowpeas/mangetout and celery go in next. Stir-fry briskly for 2 minutes.

3 Now pour in the water and flavor with a few drops of soy sauce. Toss the vegetables around in the wok or pan so that they are all coated with soy and then increase the heat if necessary to bring the water to boiling point.

4 Cover the wok or pan, reduce the heat slightly, and cook for 2-3 minutes until the vegetables are crisp but tender. Serve at once.

spicy egg-plant/ aubergine

1 pound / 450 g egg-plants/aubergines, diced

2 cloves garlic, sliced finely

1 teaspoon fresh ginger, sliced finely

4 scallions/spring onions, sliced

1 tablespoon soy sauce

1 tablespoon chili bean sauce*

1 tablespoon yellow bean sauce*

1 teaspoon sugar

1 cup / 240 ml water

oil

salt

* Available from Chinese stores and some supermarkets.

1 Sprinkle the egg-plant/aubergine cubes with salt and set aside for 15 minutes; rinse and drain.

2 Heat the oil in a wok or large pan and when it is hot put in the egg-plant/aubergine cubes. Stir them round for a couple of minutes and then put in the garlic, ginger and 2 scallions/ spring onions, cooking for 1 minute or so.

3 Now stir in the soy sauce, chili bean and yellow bean sauces, the sugar and water. Simmer, covered, for 20 minutes and serve garnished with the remaining scallions/spring onions.

tomato salad serves 4

with buttermilk

6 large tomatoes, sliced

1 medium onion, chopped finely

4 tablespoons fresh cilantro/ coriander leaves or parsley

1 fresh green chili, chopped finely or 1 teaspoon chili powder

$1/4$ teaspoon mustard powder

$1/4$ teaspoon ground cumin

$3/4$ cup / 180 ml buttermilk

1 In a salad bowl, mix everything together except the buttermilk.

2 When the ingredients are well mixed, pour on the buttermilk and stir round. Serve cold.

serves **2**

curried potato fries/chips

4 medium potatoes

oil

1/2 teaspoon turmeric

1-2 cloves garlic, crushed

1 tablespoon sesame seeds, toasted

salt

1 Start by cutting the potatoes into french fry/chip shapes. Soak them in water for 30 minutes and then drain and dry.

2 After this, heat some oil in a heavy-based pan and add the potatoes and salt. Cook for 15 minutes, stirring round.

3 Now sprinkle on the turmeric and mix it well to spread the color evenly.

4 When the potatoes are nearly done, put in the crushed garlic and sesame seeds. Stir well and then serve with dal.

serves **4**

potato pachadi

**1 pound / 450 g
potatoes, boiled and
mashed**

**¹/₂ fresh red chili,
chopped finely**

**2 teaspoons fresh ginger,
grated**

1 cup / 240 ml yogurt

salt

*Heat oven to
425°F/220°C/Gas 7*

1 Mix the chili, ginger and salt into
the mashed potato.

2 Now beat in the yogurt and mix all
the ingredients well. Turn into an
oven-proof dish and cook for 10-15
minutes or until brown.

carrots with cumin & coriander

serves **2-4**

- 1/2 pound / 225 g carrots, sliced very finely
- 1 teaspoon cumin seeds
- 1 teaspoon fresh ginger, grated
- 1/2 fresh chili, chopped finely
- 1 teaspoon ground coriander
- 1/2 teaspoon turmeric
- 1 tablespoon fresh cilantro/coriander leaves, chopped
- oil
- salt

1 Heat the oil in a pan or wok and when it is hot, sprinkle in the cumin seeds and cook for a few seconds. Then add the ginger and chili; stir.

2 Now put in the carrot slices followed by the ground coriander, turmeric and salt. Stir briskly and then cover, reduce the heat and cook for 3 minutes or until the carrots are done. Serve with the cilantro/coriander leaves sprinkled on top.

aloo gajar

serves **4-6**

spiced potatoes and carrots

1 pound / 450 g potatoes, diced and parboiled

1 pound / 450 g carrots, diced and parboiled

1 teaspoon cumin seeds

1 teaspoon ground coriander

1/2 teaspoon turmeric

a little lemon juice

1 tablespoon fresh cilantro/coriander leaves, chopped

oil

salt

1 To start, heat the oil and put in the cumin seeds. Stir these round for a few seconds before quickly adding the potatoes, stirring as you do so.

2 Now add the ground coriander and turmeric and cook on a medium heat for 3 minutes or so, stirring continuously.

3 Put in the carrots and salt at this point, and turn down the heat to low. Give the mixture a good stir and then cover and cook for 10-15 minutes.

4 Check that the potatoes and carrots are cooked and then squeeze on some lemon juice. Serve garnished with the cilantro/coriander leaves.

yogurt with tomatoes

serves **2-4**

1 teaspoon mustard seeds

6 tomatoes, sliced

1 cup / 220 ml yogurt

oil

salt

1 Heat the oil and lightly toast the mustard seeds for a few seconds, stirring.

2 Now add the tomatoes and mix them in well with the mustard seeds as they cook for 3-5 minutes.

3 Stir the yogurt into the tomato mixture; season and heat through gently without boiling and serve warm.

phulkas

makes approx **12**

flat breads

2 cups / 250 g flour
$^1/_2$ cup / 120 ml water
salt

1 Put the flour and salt into a bowl. Make a well in the middle and pour in half the water. Mix well with your hands to make a dough. If the mixture seems too dry, add more water. Shape the dough into a ball.

2 Turn the dough onto a floured board and knead it for 10-15 minutes until it becomes smooth and elastic. Then cover it with a damp cloth and set it aside for 30 minutes.

3 After this time, knead the dough again for 5 minutes. Divide it into walnut-sized pieces. Shape each piece into a ball and roll them out into rounds measuring about 5 inches/10 cm across.

4 Now lightly grease a heavy frying pan or griddle and heat it. When it is hot, place one of the dough circles on it and cook, rotating it with your fingers or a spoon, for 1-2 minutes or until bubbles appear on the top. Then flip it over and cook the other side in the same way.

5 If you have a gas cooker, grip the phulka using a metal utensil (barbecue tongs, or even nutcrackers) and hold it vertically over the flame until it puffs up. If you are using an electric stove, leave the phulka on the griddle and, using kitchen paper or a cloth, press it down firmly from all sides for a few moments. It will puff up when the pressure is released.

aloo bhaji

serves **4**

south indian potatoes

$1/4$ teaspoon powdered asafetida*

$1/4$ cup / 55 g urad dal+, soaked for 15 minutes

2 onions, sliced

1 pound / 450 g potatoes, cut into pieces and parboiled

$1/2$ teaspoon turmeric

3-4 tablespoons lemon juice

handful fresh cilantro/coriander leaves, chopped

2 tablespoons oil

salt

*Available from Asian stores. Omit if you cannot find it.

+Urad dal are the skinned, halved white insides of urad (small black beans), available in Asian stores.

1 Heat the oil in a saucepan and fry the asafetida for 10-15 seconds. Then add the onions and sauté them for a minute.

2 Put in the drained dal now and fry it with the onions for a minute or so. At the end of this time, spoon in the potatoes, sprinkle on the turmeric and salt and stir well to mix them together.

3 Cook for 5-10 minutes until the onions, potatoes and dal are soft. Then stir in the lemon juice, scatter the cilantro/coriander leaves over and serve.

sour dal

serves **4**

1 cup / 225 g toor dal

$1/_2$ teaspoon turmeric

$2^1/_2$ cups / 590 ml water

1 teaspoon tamarind*
soaked in 2 tablespoons
warm water or 2
tablespoons lemon juice

3 whole cloves

$1/_2$ teaspoon cumin seeds

$1/_2$ teaspoon fresh
ginger, grated

1 teaspoon brown sugar+

margarine or ghee

salt and pepper

+optional ingredient

*Tamarind is usually obtainable, in
block form, in Asian grocery stores.
Simply cut off what you need and
store the rest in the refrigerator.

1 Place the dal in a saucepan with the turmeric and water and bring to the boil. Then reduce the heat and cook slowly for about 30 minutes until the dal is soft and the water absorbed.

2 When the tamarind has soaked for 10 minutes, press it with a fork or spoon while still soaking to extract its juice. Then place it in a sieve over the bowl and rub with a spoon to force through the brown pulp. Pour the tamarind water, or lemon juice if using this instead, into the dal and add the seasoning.

3 Now heat the margarine or ghee in a separate pan and cook the cloves together with the cumin seeds and ginger for a few minutes.

4 Add these ingredients to the dal now and sprinkle in some sugar if using.

5 Let the dal cook very gently, or re-heat the next day. It should be quite dry but add more liquid if you wish.

mushrooms & ginger

serves **4**

³/₄ pound / 350 g mushrooms, sliced

1 tomato, chopped

¹/₂ teaspoon ground ginger

¹/₄ teaspoon turmeric

1 tablespoon fennel leaves, chopped*

¹/₄ teaspoon chili powder

oil

salt

*Or use parsley, dill or cilantro/coriander leaves.

1 Heat the oil and when it is hot put in the mushroom slices. Stir as you fry them for 3 minutes until they are evenly soft and cooked.

2 Now add the tomato, ginger, turmeric and fennel leaves and chili. Mix well and season, and continue to cook until the tomato has integrated.

spinach & potato bhaji

serves **4-6**

$^3/_4$ pound / 350 g
potatoes, diced and
parboiled

2 pounds / 1 kg spinach,
chopped finely

1 onion, chopped finely

1 green chili,
chopped finely

$^1/_2$ teaspoon turmeric

$^1/_2$ teaspoon ground
mixed spice

$^1/_2$ cup / 110 g curd or
cottage cheese

oil or ghee

salt

1 Using a wok, heat the oil or ghee and then lightly fry the potatoes to golden brown. Remove and keep warm.

2 Next, using more fat as necessary, fry the onion and chili until the onion begins to soften.

3 Now add the spinach, turmeric and ground mixed spice. Turn up the heat and then stir as the spinach cooks down, taking about 5 minutes.

4 After that put in the curd or cottage cheese, the potatoes and salt. Stir and cook gently for a further 5-10 minutes until the spinach has crumpled and most of the liquid has evaporated.

INDONESIA

nasi minyak

serves **4**

fragrant rice

1 onion, sliced finely

2 cloves garlic, crushed

1 teaspoon turmeric

1/2 teaspoon five-spice powder*

2 tablespoons almond flakes

1 cup / 225 g rice

2 tablespoons ghee, margarine or oil

1 1/2 cups / 350 ml water

salt

*Obtainable from Chinese stores. If you cannot obtain this, then use the same quantity of ground mixed spice.

1 Heat the oil in a large saucepan and then sauté the onion and garlic for a few minutes until they soften.

2 Now put in the turmeric, spice powder, 1 tablespoon of the almond flakes and salt and cook for a little longer.

3 Add the rice and fry it for 2-3 minutes, stirring all the time. When you have done this, pour in the water and bring the pan to the boil, giving the rice an occasional stir.

4 Once it is boiling, cover the pot and turn down the heat as low as possible while maintaining a simmering heat. Cook the rice until all the liquid has been absorbed and the grains are fluffy. If necessary, add more water.

5 Just before serving, scatter the remaining almond flakes over the top.

INDONESIA

peppery potatoes

serves **2**

2 tablespoons oil

1 small onion, sliced

1/2 teaspoon chili powder

1/2 teaspoon mustard powder

1/2 teaspoon turmeric

1/2 inch / 1 cm fresh ginger root, peeled and grated

2 medium potatoes, diced and parboiled

1 medium egg-plant/ aubergine, sliced thinly

salt

1 Heat the oil in a pan and cook the onion until it is clear and soft.

2 After that put in the chili, salt, mustard, turmeric and ginger. Then add the partly-cooked potatoes and egg-plant/aubergine and lightly brown them all over, turning constantly to prevent them catching.

3 Add just enough water to come half-way up the vegetables, cover the pan and cook gently until the vegetables are tender and the liquid is absorbed.

yang bai chuna mool

serves **4**

marinated cabbage salad

$^1/_2$ pound / 225 g chinese cabbage or equivalent, chopped finely

1 tablespoon sesame seeds

6 inch / 15 cm cucumber

$1^1/_2$ tablespoons sesame oil

1 inch / 2.5 cm fresh ginger root, peeled and grated

$^1/_2$ tablespoon sugar

2 scallions / spring onions, chopped very finely

$1^1/_2$ tablespoons white wine vinegar

2 tablespoons light soy sauce

$^1/_2$-1 fresh green chili, or chili powder to taste

1 To start, toast the sesame seeds in a pan with a minimum of oil until they are golden and beginning to jump. Remove and allow to cool.

2 After this, cut the cucumber in half and then slice it into thin lengthwise strips. Now put the cucumber pieces, together with the chinese cabbage, into a salad bowl.

3 Using a small bowl or cup, mix together the oil, ginger, sugar, scallions/spring onions, vinegar, sesame seeds, soy sauce and chili. Pour this over the salad and stir well. Then leave it to marinate for 5 hours if possible before serving.

pagri terong

serves **4**

fried egg-plant/aubergine

1 pound / 450 g egg-plants/aubergines, sliced lengthwise

4 scallions/spring onions, sliced

2 cloves garlic, crushed

$1/2$ fresh green chili, sliced finely

$1/2$ fresh red chili, sliced finely

1 teaspoon fresh ginger, grated

1 teaspoon ground cumin

seeds from 3 black cardamoms, crushed

1 inch / 2.5 cm cinnamon stick

1 teaspoon fennel seeds, crushed

2 teaspoons mild curry powder

1 cup / 240 ml coconut milk

oil

salt

1 In a wok or large pan, heat up the oil and when it is very hot quickly sauté the egg-plants/aubergines. Stir them round and when they start browning and softening, remove from the pan, drain and cool.

2 Now, using the same oil (adding more if required), fry the scallions/spring onions for 30 seconds. Add the garlic and cook together for a few moments.

3 When these are beginning to soften, put in the chili and ginger, frying everything together for 1 minute.

4 Then add the cumin, cardamom seeds, cinnamon, fennel seeds and curry powder. Stir-fry for 2-3 minutes before pouring on the coconut milk. Season with salt and then return the egg-plants/aubergines and cook gently for 5-10 minutes until the mixture thickens.

palak ka baghara salan

serves **4**

spinach with chili

2 pounds / 1 kg spinach, chopped	1 green chili, finely sliced
2 cloves garlic, crushed	$^1/_2$ teaspoon turmeric
1 teaspoon fresh ginger, chopped finely	a little water
1 onion, finely sliced	oil
	salt

1 Mix the garlic and ginger together to make a paste.

2 Now heat the oil and fry the onion until it becomes translucent. Add the ginger and garlic paste and stir fry for another minute or two.

3 Next add the chili and stir it into the onion mixture, cooking for 30 seconds.

4 When this is done, shake in the turmeric and salt. Mix everything well before adding the spinach. Stir this in, add a little water and then cover the pan. Simmer over a gentle heat until the spinach is soft and the moisture has evaporated.

serves **4-6**

kilowin talong sa gata

grilled egg-plant/aubergine salad

1 pound / 450 g egg-plants/aubergines, sliced*

3 tomatoes, chopped

1 scallion/spring onion, chopped finely

2 tablespoons vinegar

1/2 tablespoon black peppercorns, crushed

1/2 cup / 120 ml coconut milk

salt

*The slender ones are best, but the larger purple ones will do.

1 First place the tomatoes, scallion/spring onion, peppercorns and vinegar into a bowl and mix well. Set aside for 1 hour.

2 When ready to make the salad, grill the egg-plant/aubergine slices until they are soft.

3 Place the pieces in a salad bowl and cover them with the tomato mixture. Set aside for 30 minutes.

4 Now pour the coconut milk over the salad; season and toss the ingredients lightly to mix well.

mint & cilantro/ coriander chutney

2 tablespoons fresh cilantro/coriander leaves, chopped

1 tablespoon fresh mint leaves, chopped

1 clove garlic, crushed

1 green chili, finely chopped or ground

1 tablespoon lemon juice

1 tablespoon yogurt or thick coconut milk

salt

1 Put all the ingredients into a blender and whizz for a few seconds to mix well. Add more yogurt or coconut milk as desired to make the consistency you prefer.

makes **12**

coconut rotis

coconut bread

2 cups / 250 g flour

1¹/₂ cups / 150 g desiccated coconut

a little ghee or margarine

salt

1 To begin, gently warm the flour in a pan over a low heat.

2 Then mix it with the coconut in a basin and add a little boiling water to make a thick paste.

3 Shape this mixture into balls the size of an egg and then flatten them to the size of a saucer.

4 Put a little ghee or margarine in a pan and cook the first roti on one side for about 1 minute, then turn it over and cook for a further minute. When it is done, remove it and keep warm while you repeat the process with the remaining rotis. Serve as soon as possible after cooking.

pepina saladeh

serves **6**

cucumber salad

3 cups / 300 g cucumber, sliced	**3 small red onions, sliced**
2-4 teaspoons salt	**a few drops anchovy essence***
½ cup / 120 ml water	
2 teaspoons pepper	**juice of 1 orange**
1-2 green chilis, sliced thinly	*optional ingredient

1 Start by putting the cucumber slices into a bowl. Then stir the salt into the water and pour this over the cucumber, mixing well and pressing the cucumber slices a little as you do it. Leave to soak for 30 minutes.

2 After this time, squeeze the water from the cucumber slices and add the other ingredients. Mix well, and chill before serving.

serves **4-6**

tomato chutney

1 cup / 240 ml vinegar

2 dried red chilis, soaked in the vinegar for 2 hours

2 cloves garlic, crushed

$^1/_2$ teaspoon fresh ginger, grated

2 tablespoons sugar or to taste

1 pound / 450 g tomatoes, sliced

$^1/_2$ cup / 50 g dates, stoned and chopped

salt

FOR THE SPICE POWDER (1 teaspoon) – crush these and mix together:

2 cloves

seeds from 5 cardamom pods

$^1/_2$ inch / 1.5 cm piece of cinnamon

1 Remove the chilis from the vinegar, retaining this for later use. Grind the soaked chilis with the ginger and garlic in a blender.

2 Now put the vinegar, sugar and salt into a large pan and bring to the boil.

3 At this point, add the tomatoes, dates and the teaspoon of spice powder. Stir them round and then simmer on a moderate heat until the mixture becomes very thick and has the consistency you like for chutney.

4 Remove the pan from the heat, allow to cool a little and then spoon the chutney into warmed jars. Cover and once opened, store in the refrigerator for up to 6 weeks.

latin
america
& caribbean

BRAZIL

tutu

black beans

Ingredients	

1 cup / 225 g black kidney beans, cooked

2 tablespoons flour

water

1 bayleaf

1/4 teaspoon chili powder

salt and pepper

FOR THE TOPPING

1 onion, chopped

1 bell pepper, thinly sliced

1/2 chili, finely chopped

2 tomatoes, sliced

1 tablespoon fresh cilantro/coriander leaves, chopped

oil

salt and pepper

Heat oven to 350°F/180°C/Gas 4

1 Place the cooked beans in a blender or bowl and mash them using a fork. Transfer them to a saucepan.

2 Sift the flour into a bowl and pour in enough water to make a runny paste. Add this to the beans, together with the bayleaf, chili powder, and seasoning.

3 Now warm up the mixture very slowly, stirring from time to time, until it forms a smooth paste. Let this cook for 5 minutes and then transfer to an ovenproof dish.

4 To prepare the topping, heat the oil and gently cook the onion, bell pepper and chili for a few minutes. Add the tomatoes and half the cilantro/coriander leaves and cook for a further few minutes.

5 Spoon the topping onto the bean mixture and bake in the oven for 10 minutes. Garnish with the remaining cilantro/coriander leaves before serving.

112 LATIN AMERICA **&** CARIBBEAN

salade à la caraïbe

serves **4**

caribbean salad

1 cup / 110 g white cabbage, shredded

1 cup / 100 g cucumber, grated

1 red bell pepper, finely sliced in circles

1 mango, peeled, stoned and sliced

4-6 scallions/spring onions, chopped

1/2-1 avocado pear, peeled and sliced

1 clove garlic, crushed

juice of 1-2 limes or lemons

4-6 tablespoons olive oil

1 handful watercress

salt and pepper

1 First, arrange the cabbage, cucumber, bell pepper, mango and scallions/spring onions in a salad bowl.

2 Now put in half the avocado slices.

3 Then blend the garlic with the lime or lemon juice, olive oil and salt and pepper. Pour half the dressing over and toss the salad.

4 Now arrange the cress and remaining avocado slices on top and drizzle the rest of the dressing over before serving.

pumpkin & cashew nut salad

serves **2**

2 cups / 300 g pumpkin, cubed and boiled or steamed for 10 minutes

¼ cup / 30 g cashew nuts, lightly toasted

4 tablespoons oil-and-vinegar dressing/ vinaigrette

slices of watermelon and green bell pepper for garnish or use tomato and parsley

salt and pepper

1 When the cooked pumpkin has cooled a little, mix the cubes carefully with the vinaigrette so that all the pieces are coated. Keep a few of the toasted cashews back for garnish and combine the rest into the pumpkin salad and season.

2 Now pile the salad back into the pumpkin shell or serving bowl and decorate with the watermelon and bell pepper slices or tomato and parsley before serving.

CHILE

tomato
salad

serves **2-3**

**4 tomatoes, sliced
thinly in circles**

**1 onion, sliced
thinly in circles**

**1 tablespoon
parsley, chopped**

¹/₂ tablespoon oil

¹/₂ teaspoon chili powder

salt and pepper

1 Mix together the tomatoes, onions and parsley with the oil. Season with salt and pepper.

2 Serve on a shallow dish with the chili sprinkled on top.

CHILE

sopaipillas

serves **2-4**

pumpkin cakes

$^1/_2$ **pound / 225 g pumpkin, chopped into 1 inch/2.5 cm chunks**

1 cup / 225 g flour

1 teaspoon baking powder

1 teaspoon ground cinnamon

$^1/_2$ **tablespoon margarine**

salt

Heat oven to 400°F/200°C/Gas 6

1 First boil the pumpkin chunks until soft. Drain and then mash them in a mixing bowl with a little salt and margarine.

2 Now sieve in the flour, baking powder, and cinnamon; add the margarine and salt and mix the ingredients together.

3 Shape the dough into a ball and press it out on a floured surface to a thickness of $1/4$ inch/$1/2$ cm. Then cut out portions with a cup or pastry cutter.

4 Arrange the pumpkin cakes on a greased baking tray, prick with a fork, and bake for 20 minutes or until golden.

ensalada de coliflor

serves **4**

cauliflower salad

**1 cauliflower, cooked
whole and cooled**

1 large ripe avocado

**1 tablespoon white wine
vinegar or lemon juice**

2-3 tablespoons oil

**1/4 cup / 50 g ground
almonds**

a little milk

salt and pepper

1 To start with, place the whole cauliflower into a serving dish. If preferred you can carefully cut off the florets and arrange these on their own in the dish.

2 Now slice open the avocado, remove the stone and scoop the flesh into a mixing bowl. Mash the avocado, adding the vinegar or lemon juice, oil, milk, ground almonds and seasoning, until you have a smooth coating sauce.

3 Spoon this over the cauliflower and serve immediately.

serves **2-4**

avocado salad

1 large ripe avocado

4 slices fresh pineapple, or a medium can, drained

2 tablespoons olive oil

$1/_2$-1 tablespoon lemon juice

a few lettuce leaves

a little chopped parsley

salt and pepper

NOTE: Add tuna, nuts or cottage cheese to make a more substantial meal.

1 Start by slicing round the avocado to open it and taking out the stone. Then peel off the skin and cut the flesh into small pieces.

2 Remove the skin from the fresh pineapple and cut the fruit into chunks. If using tuna, cottage cheese or nuts, place these in a bowl with the avocado.

3 In a separate container whisk the olive oil, lemon juice, salt and pepper with a fork to make the dressing.

4 Pour this over the salad and stir gently. Place the lettuce leaves on a flat dish and cover them with the avocado and pineapple mixture, garnishing with parsley. Serve with hot bread, potatoes or cracked wheat.

spicy pumpkin

serves **4**

1 onion, finely sliced

1-2 cloves garlic, crushed

2 teaspoons curry powder

3 cloves, crushed

1/2 red chili, finely chopped

1 pound / 450 g pumpkin, peeled and cut into 1 inch/ 2.5 cm cubes

2 tomatoes, chopped

1 tablespoon sultanas

1/4 teaspoon sugar*

juice of 1 lemon

2 tablespoons oil

salt and pepper

*optional ingredient

1 First, heat the oil in a heavy pan and then add the onion. Sauté until it is transparent and then add the garlic and cook that also.

2 Next put in the curry powder, ground cloves and chili and cook for a further 2 minutes.

3 When this is done, add the pumpkin chunks, the chopped tomatoes, the sultanas and sugar. Sprinkle the lemon juice over.

4 Cover, and cook very gently for 30-40 minutes or until the pumpkin is tender, stirring frequently to ensure that it does not catch. Season and serve to accompany main dishes and rice.

MEXICO

tortillas

serves **12**

1 cup / 150 g fine cornmeal

1 cup / 125 g wheat flour

1¹/₂ cups / 360 ml warm water

a little oil

1 Put the cornmeal and flour in a bowl and add enough water to make a dough. Knead this well until it is smooth and elastic, and then divide it into 12 pieces.

2 Cut 2 pieces of aluminum foil or waxed/greaseproof paper into 8 inch/20 cm squares and grease these lightly.

3 Put a ball of the dough between the paper/foil and roll it with a rolling pin into a 6 inch/15 cm circle.

4 Next, heat a lightly-greased heavy, shallow pan. Remove one of the layers of paper/foil and place the tortilla in the pan, with its remaining paper/foil side uppermost. Cook for about 1 minute.

5 Remove the paper/foil and turn the tortilla over to cook the other side. Both sides should be dry with brown patches.

6 Stack the tortillas, cover to keep warm and serve as soon as possible.

berros salad <small>serves **4-6**</small>

1/2 pound / 225 g cress/watercress

10 red radishes, topped and tailed

4-6 tablespoons olive oil

2 tablespoons vinegar

salt

1 Separate out the cress strands and place them in a salad bowl.

2 Cut the radishes into thin, round slices and then mix most of them in with the cress, retaining some for a garnish.

3 Now join the olive oil to the vinegar and mix well with the salad, adding salt. Decorate with the remaining radish slices before placing in the refrigerator for about 2 hours until required.

casserole

serves **4-6**

with egg-plant/aubergine

1 pound / 450 g egg-plant/aubergine, cut into ¹/₂ inch/ 1 cm slices

1 tablespoon oil

1 medium onion, finely chopped

1-2 cloves garlic, crushed

1 red or green bell pepper, chopped finely

1 green chili or ¹/₂ teaspoon chili powder

¹/₂ teaspoon ground cumin

5 tablespoons tomato paste

³/₄ cup / 180 ml water

2 cups / 225 g cheddar cheese, grated

salt and pepper

Heat oven to 400°F/200°C/Gas 6

1 First of all, place the egg-plant/ aubergine slices in a single layer on a greased baking sheet and bake uncovered in the oven for 10-20 minutes until soft.

2 Now heat the oil in a pan and sauté the onion, garlic and bell pepper for 5 minutes. Then add the chili, cumin, tomato paste and continue to cook for 3 minutes before pouring in the water.

3 Bring to the boil, stirring from time to time and then lower the heat and simmer, uncovered, for 10 minutes. Add salt and pepper to taste.

4 In a shallow greased oven-proof dish, put a layer of the egg-plant/ aubergine slices and spoon on half the sauce. Sprinkle half of the cheese on top. Repeat with the remaining ingredients.

5 Bake, uncovered, for 15-20 minutes. Serve with baked sweet potatoes.

pererreque

corn/maize cake

1 pound / 450 g fine white corn / maize meal

1 pound / 450 g crumbly cheese, grated finely (try monterrey jack or wensleydale)

1 cup / 200 g sugar

2 tablespoons / 25 g margarine

1/2 teaspoon bicarbonate of soda

2 1/2 cups / 590 ml milk

Heat oven to 350°F/180°C/Gas 4

1 First mix the corn/maize meal together with the cheese and sugar in a bowl. Then rub in the margarine.

2 Now mix the bicarbonate of soda into a little of the milk and pour this into the other ingredients. Then add more milk to make a mixture which is soft enough to find its own level when spooned into a cake tin. Mix well.

3 Place the cake mixture into a baking tray or cake tin. The mixture should be about 1 inch/2.5 cm thick.

4 Bake for 30-40 minutes until the cake is golden brown. After this time, remove it from the oven, allow to cool and then cut into small pieces or squares before serving cold.

PARAGUAY

sopa paraguaya

paraguayan corn bread

1 can creamed corn kernels	3 eggs
¹/₂ cup / 75 g corn/maize meal	1 tablespoon flour
²/₃ cup / 150 ml milk	1 tablespoon butter or margarine
2 cups / 200 g cheddar or monterrey jack cheese, grated	4 tablespoons oil
1 onion, finely chopped	salt

Heat oven to
400°F/200°C/Gas 6

1 First, grease a 8 inch/20 cm square baking tin or dish. Sprinkle on some flour and then tap the tin to remove the excess.

2 Now put the corn kernels into a bowl with the corn/maize meal, milk, cheese and a little salt. Add 3 tablespoons of the oil and mix everything well.

3 Next heat up the remaining tablespoon of oil in a pan and sauté the onion; then add this to the corn mixture.

4 When this is done, separate the eggs and whisk the whites until they are stiff. Now beat the yolks and gently fold them into the whites.

5 Spoon the blended eggs into the corn mixture and then pour this into the baking dish and dot with butter or margarine. Bake for about 45 minutes.

egg-plant/ aubergine

serves **2**

with pimiento dressing

1/2 pound / 225 g egg-plants/aubergines, cubed

1 clove garlic, crushed

1 tablespoon lime or lemon juice

1 scallion/spring onion, chopped finely

1 stick celery, chopped finely

a few lettuce leaves

salt

FOR THE DRESSING:

1 cup / 100 g pimientos, drained

1 tablespoon white vinegar

1 teaspoon mustard

1/4 cup / 60 ml buttermilk or milk

1 To prepare the egg-plants/aubergines, place the chunks in a pan and barely cover with water. Bring to the boil before adding the garlic, lime or lemon juice and salt. Simmer for about 10 minutes until just tender and then drain and set aside to cool.

2 While that is happening, make the dressing by putting all the ingredients into a blender and adding enough buttermilk or milk to make a smooth sauce.

3 Now mix the cooled egg-plants/aubergines with the onion and celery, adding salt. Place the lettuce leaves on a serving dish and spoon on the mixture. Cover with the dressing and serve.

middle
east &
north
africa

egg-plant/ aubergine salad

serves **4**

1 pound / 450 g egg-plants/aubergines

2 cloves garlic, crushed

1/2 teaspoon cayenne pepper or chili powder

1 teaspoon ground cumin

1 teaspoon paprika

1 tablespoon lemon juice

1 tablespoon fresh parsley, chopped

1 tomato, cut into wedges

oil

salt and pepper

Heat oven to 200°F/400°C/Gas 6

1 Put the egg-plants/aubergines, whole, onto a baking tray and prick the skins. Bake for 20 minutes or until very soft. Set aside to cool.

2 Next, place the flesh in a bowl. Chop and then mash with a fork. Add the garlic, cayenne or chili powder, cumin, half the paprika, and seasoning. Add the lemon juice and mix well.

3 Now heat some oil in a heavy pan and cook the mashed egg-plant/ aubergine mix, stirring all the time until it has browned.

4 Transfer to a serving dish, sprinkle with remaining paprika, the parsley and a few drops of oil. Decorate with the tomato wedges.

EGYPT

stuffed tomatoes

serves **4-6**

with bulghur or cracked wheat

$^1/_2$ cup / 110 g cracked wheat or bulghur, cooked

6 big tomatoes

3 tablespoons olive oil

1-2 tablespoons lemon juice

4 small tomatoes

handful of chives, parsley and fresh mint, chopped

6 scallions/spring onions or 1 medium onion, sliced finely

a few lettuce leaves

salt and pepper

1 To start, cut the tops off the big tomatoes and scoop out the seeds and pulp (keep these). Make the dressing by mixing the oil, lemon juice, salt and pepper in a bowl.

2 Next, take the skins off the small tomatoes by putting them in a bowl and pouring boiling water over them. The skins will split and can easily be removed. Cut these tomatoes into small cubes and add to the chopped pulp from the large tomatoes.

3 Now mix the tomatoes, wheat, chopped herbs and scallions/spring onions with the dressing. Fill the big tomatoes with this mixture and arrange them on a bed of lettuce leaves.

IRAQ

roz bil tamar serves 4

rice with dates and almonds

1 cup / 125 g almonds

1 cup / 100 g dates, stoned

1 cup / 100 g sultanas or raisins

1 teaspoon rose water or a little grated orange rind

1 cup / 225 g rice, cooked

2 tablespoons margarine

salt

1 Melt the margarine in a large pan and when it is gently bubbling, add the almonds. Fry them, stirring often, for one or two minutes.

2 Next put in the dates and sultanas or raisins, adding more margarine if necessary. Keep stirring so that nothing sticks or burns, and cook for a few minutes until the dried fruit begins to plump up.

3 Now heap the rice on top of the fruit and nut mixture; cover. Cook over a very gentle heat, or place in a low oven, for 10–20 minutes to let everything heat through.

4 Just before serving, sprinkle on the rose water and garnish with additional almonds and orange peel.

IRAN

borani esfanaj

serves **4**

spinach and yogurt salad

1 onion, finely chopped

2 cloves garlic, crushed

1 pound / 450 g spinach, chopped

1 cup / 220 g yogurt

2 tablespoons oil

salt and pepper

1 Heat the oil and sauté the onion for several minutes until it is golden. Then add the garlic and after a minute or two, put in the spinach and seasoning.

2 Cook the spinach, turning from time to time, until it has settled and softened. Transfer it to a serving dish and let it cool.

3 When ready to serve, blend in the yogurt and mix well.

tabbouli

serves **4-6**

bulghur wheat salad

½ cup / 110 g bulghur

a few lettuce leaves

4 tablespoons fresh parsley, chopped

2 tablespoons fresh mint, chopped

1 onion, finely sliced

4 tomatoes, chopped

4 tablespoons lemon juice

4 tablespoons olive oil

salt and pepper

1 First, soak the bulghur for 20 minutes or so in enough cold water to cover. Then drain well.

2 Line a salad bowl with the lettuce leaves and then spoon in the bulghur. Scatter in 3 tablespoons of the parsley together with the mint, onion and tomatoes and mix them in.

3 Now join the lemon juice to the oil, season with salt and pepper and mix well. Pour this over and toss the salad to coat the ingredients evenly. Sprinkle the remaining spoonful of parsley on top.

fava pâté

serves **4**

broad bean pâté

1 pound / 450 g broad beans (canned or frozen will do)

2 cloves garlic, crushed

1/2 teaspoon chili powder

juice of 1/2 lemon

1 tablespoon fresh parsley, chopped

2 tablespoons olive oil

salt

1 If using fresh or frozen beans, put them into a saucepan containing boiling water and cook for a few minutes until tender; drain.

2 Now mix the garlic and chili powder in a bowl together with the salt. Add the beans to this mixture and mash them with a fork or use a blender. Combine all the ingredients well and transfer to a small shallow dish.

3 Combine the lemon juice and olive oil and pour over; scatter the fresh parsley on top. Serve with hot pitta bread.

LIBYA

olive salad

serves **2-4**

1 cup / 150 g green
olives

1 cup / 150 g
black olives

juice of 1 lemon

2 tablespoons
parsley, chopped

1 teaspoon paprika

$1/4$ teaspoon chili powder

1 clove garlic, crushed

$1/2$ teaspoon ground
cumin

2 tablespoons oil

1 In a bowl, mix the oil with the cumin, chili powder, paprika, parsley, garlic and lemon juice. Then pour this dressing over the olives in a bowl and stir round so that they are well coated.

2 Put the salad in the fridge to chill before serving.

fasolyeh bi ban banadoora

serves **4**

beans with tomatoes

1 onion, finely sliced

1 pound / 450 g green beans (french, runner or string beans), cut into 1 inch/2.5 cm pieces

$^1/_2$ teaspoon allspice

$^1/_2$ teaspoon ground cumin

2-3 tomatoes, chopped

1 cup / 225 g yogurt

2 tablespoons oil

salt and pepper

1 Heat the oil and sauté the onion. Then put in the beans, allspice, cumin and seasoning. Reduce the heat, cover the pan and cook for 5 minutes or so.

2 After this, remove the cover and throw in the tomatoes. Continue to cook until they are tender. Serve with yogurt.

salatah arabiyeh

serves **4-6**

arab salad

1 green bell pepper, sliced thinly

1 small onion, sliced finely

3 tomatoes, cut into thin wedges

4 radishes, cut into thin rounds

1 clove garlic, chopped finely

2 tablespoons parsley, chopped finely

4-5 cilantro/coriander seeds, crushed or $\frac{1}{2}$ teaspoon ground cilantro/coriander

3 tablespoons olive oil

juice of 1 lemon

salt and pepper

1 In a salad bowl, mix all the ingredients together except the olive oil and lemon juice.

2 Now combine these two and pour over the salad, turning it gently to distribute the dressing before serving.

MOROCCO

potato with cumin

serves **4-6**

2 pounds / 1 kg potatoes, cut into chunks and parboiled

1 red or green bell pepper, cut into thin strips

2 cloves garlic, crushed

1 tablespoon ground cumin

peel of $1/2$ lemon, thinly sliced

2 tablespoons parsley, chopped

oil

salt and pepper

1 To start, heat the oil in a heavy pan and fry the bell pepper until it softens. Then add the garlic and cumin and blend these by stirring as they cook.

2 Now add the potatoes and turn them round in the oil so that they brown on all sides.

3 When they are almost ready, sprinkle in the lemon peel and mix in with the other ingredients. Season.

4 Scatter the parsley on top just before serving, with yogurt to accompany the dish.

egg-plant/ aubergine & tomatoes

serves **4**

1 pound / 450 g egg-plants/aubergines, sliced

1 onion, sliced

2 cloves garlic, crushed

1 green bell pepper, finely sliced

4 tomatoes, sliced

¹/₄ teaspoon chili powder

1 teaspoon ground cumin

1 tablespoon lemon juice

oil

salt and pepper

1 First heat the oil in a large pan and then sauté the onion until it turns golden.

2 Now add the garlic, bell pepper and egg-plant/aubergine slices. Turn the slices from time to time as they cook for 10 minutes.

3 When the bell pepper and egg-plant/aubergine slices are soft, put in the tomatoes, the chili powder and cumin and season with salt and pepper. Stir the ingredients and simmer gently for 20 minutes.

4 Sprinkle on some lemon juice before serving.

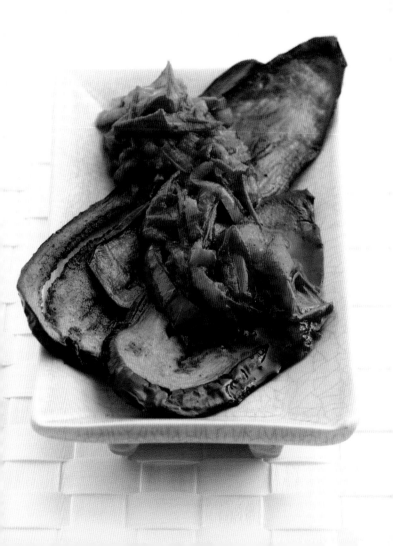

salade de zalouk

serves **4**

spicy vegetable salad

½ teaspoon chili powder	**1** First heat the oil and put in the chili powder, garlic and a little salt.
2 cloves garlic, crushed	
1 egg-plant/aubergine, cut into cubes	**2** Next, sauté the egg-plant/aubergine cubes for a few minutes, followed by the zucchini/courgettes and then the bell peppers.
2 zucchini/courgettes, sliced	
2 red or green bell peppers, sliced	**3** Add the tomatoes and chili now and cook without the lid, stirring frequently, until all the vegetables have amalgamated and most of the liquid has evaporated.
4 tomatoes, chopped	
½ chili, chopped	**4** Check the flavors and seasoning and adjust to taste. Transfer the salad to a bowl and allow to cool before serving.
4 tablespoons oil	
salt and pepper	

nutrition facts

With increasing concern about obesity in the West, and poor nutrition in many Majority World countries, it is useful to know what we require from our food – and what we do not need. Buying fair trade and organic produce improves the quality of what we eat while also supporting ethical farming and trading practices.

Humans need carbohydrates, fiber, protein, fat, vitamins and minerals as well as water. These maintain our bodies and give us energy, measured in calories. A person's calorie requirement varies according to their age, health, size and activity level. A small person with a sedentary life may only require 2,000 calories a day, while someone who is large and does heavy physical work may need 3,500. The UN agencies recommend a minimum daily intake (RDI) for adults of 2,300-2,600 calories per person.

Ideally, calories should be drawn from the range of nutrients listed above. The main or macro-nutrients – carbohydrates, protein and fat – provide different amounts of calories. Fat is very high in calories: one gram of oil, butter or margarine supplies nine calories. Carbohydrates (from sugars and starches) and protein (from beans, nuts and dairy foods) provide four calories for each gram. Alcohol delivers seven calories per gram (or milliliter), so a glass of dry white wine would be about 100 calories.

Protein

Protein is the body's building material. It is made up of amino acids; foods contain these in differing proportions. The highest-quality protein foods contain the most complete set of essential amino acids in the right proportions for the body to be able to make the best use of them. According to the American Dietetics Association, 'plant sources of protein alone can provide adequate amounts of essential amino acids if a variety of plant foods are consumed and energy needs are met.' The UN Food and Agriculture Organization recommends that around 10 per cent of a person's energy intake should come from protein. So on the 2,600 RDI calories about 260 should be from protein. Since each gram of protein provides four calories, you would therefore need 65 grams of protein each day, depending on your age, sex, lifestyle and so on. The UN figure leaves a comfortable margin: the Vegetarian Society in Britain suggests that 45 grams per day is plenty for women (more if pregnant, breastfeeding or very active) and 55 grams for men (more if very active).

People in the rich world rarely lack protein because overall we consume well above the 2,600 calories level and within that food intake there is likely to be sufficient protein. It is a different situation in countries where the overall calorie consumption is low (the 500 million people of the least developed countries rarely consume more than 2,000 calories; one of the lowest national averages is Sierra Leone's 1,880).

Vegetarian foods rich in protein include nuts, seeds, pulses (peas, beans, lentils), grains, dairy produce, eggs and soy products such as tofu. Vegetables, salads and fruit contribute small amounts of amino acids as well.

Carbohydrates
Carbohydrates are the main source of energy. In plant foods, these normally come as sugars and starches. Avoid sugars and refined starches (white bread, white rice) as although they bring

calories, they bring few nutrients. By contrast, cereals such as wholemeal bread, pasta, oats and root vegetables like potatoes and parsnips, bring nourishment along with the same amount of calories. They also provide fiber or roughage.

Fats and oils
In the West we consume a lot of energy as fat and sugar, in processed and fast foods (cakes, biscuits, ice-cream, chips and pies). This can result in heart disease and obesity, illnesses which kill around 2.5 million people each year.

A little fat is essential to keep body tissues healthy, for the manufacture of hormones and to carry the vitamins A, D, E and K. Fats are made up of fatty acids. There are saturated and unsaturated fats, referring to how much hydrogen they contain.

Saturated fats, found mainly in animal products, contain cholesterol. Our bodies need this but can produce what they require. Excess cholesterol can clog arteries, leading to increased risk of heart disease. Saturated fats raise blood cholesterol levels while unsaturated fats – such as olive and sunflower oil – lower them.

WHO advises between 15-30 per cent of total energy intake as fat, with no more than 10 per cent of it in the form of saturated fat. So if your calorie intake is 2,600, and 20 per cent of this comes from fat, that would give 520 calories. Since each gram of fat brings nine calories, this means you should eat about 58 g or two ounces a day. The West's daily average is double that, contributing 1,080 calories before adding those from protein and carbohydrates.

Dairy products are laden with saturated fat, especially hard cheeses, cream and whole milk. Choose low-fat yogurt, cottage or low-fat cheese and skimmed milk that also deliver useful protein. Plant foods rich in fats – avocado pears, nuts and seeds – should be eaten in moderation. Unlike crisps or French fries, however, nuts and seeds do also provide protein, vitamins and a substantial amount of fiber. Pulses, whole grains, vegetables and fruit are low in fat.

Vitamins
These are nutrients that the body cannot produce for itself either at all or in sufficient quantities. Vitamins are essential for growth, cell repair and regulating metabolism (the rate at which the body consumes energy). Green leafy vegetables are a major source of many vitamins and minerals – try to eat them uncooked when you can.

Minerals
These keep the body functioning properly. Calcium, iron, potassium and magnesium are the main minerals; others such as zinc and iodine are known as trace elements and are needed only in tiny amounts. ■

fair trade food

Fairly traded (and organic) products are becoming widely available. If you can't find them where you shop, keep asking. Even giant supermarkets have to listen to their customers. They have huge power over producers; this is part of the problem with 'free' trade. So shopping in smaller stores, or through aid organizations, is a good way to support fair trade. The products cost a little more, because fair trade producers are paid above the cost of production.

The price of almost all food commodities from the South has been falling to below production cost, thus impoverishing farmers while traders and retailers have prospered.

Where to buy?
Fair trade food products are available from alternative outlets, see below.

The International Federation for Alternative Trade (IFAT)
A network of fair trade organizations, many of them Southern producers. They have agreed common objectives:
● To improve the livelihoods of producers ● To promote development opportunities for disadvantaged producers ● To raise consumer awareness ● To set an example of partnership in trade ● To campaign for changes in conventional trade ● To protect human rights.
www.ifat.org

IFAT members who sell some of the food products for the recipes in this book:
Australia
Community Aid Abroad Trading:
www.caatrading.org.au
Britain
Traidcraft Exchange:
www.traidcraft.co.uk

Canada
Level Ground Trading Ltd:
www.levelground.com

Japan
Global Village Fair Trade Company:
www.globalvillage.org.jp

New Zealand/Aotearoa
Trade Aid Importers Ltd:
www.tradeaid.org.nz

US
Equal Exchange:
www.equalexchange.com

Fair Trade Labelling Organizations International (FLO)
Most national fair trade labels are now members of FLO. Their common principles include:

• Democratic organization of production • Unrestricted access to free trade unions • No child labor • Decent working conditions • A price that covers the costs of production • Long-term relationships • A social premium to improve conditions • Environmental sustainability

The FLO monitoring program ensures that the trading partners comply with fair trade criteria and that individual producers benefit.

Most national fair trade labels adopt the main elements of a common logo (left). **www.fairtrade.net**

Britain
The Fairtrade Foundation:
www.fairtrade.org.uk

Canada
TransFair:
www.web.net/fairtrade

Europe
Max Havelaar:
www.maxhavelaar.nl
TransFair: www.transfair.org

Ireland
Fairtrade Mark Ireland:
www.fair-mark.org

US
TransFair:
www.transfairusa.org

Japan
TransFair:
www.transfair-jp.com

index

173

about the new internationalist

www.newint.org

New Internationalist Publications is a co-operative with offices in Oxford (England), Adelaide (Australia), Toronto (Canada) and Christchurch (New Zealand/Aotearoa). The monthly **New Internationalist** magazine now has more than 75,000 subscribers worldwide. In addition to the magazine and the **One World Almanac**, the co-operative also publishes the **One World Calendar**, an outstanding collection of full-colour photographs. It also publishes books, including: the successful series of **No-Nonsense Guides** to the key issues in the world today; cookbooks containing recipes and cultural information from around the world; and photographic books on topics such as Nomadic Peoples and Water. The **NI** is the English-language publisher of the biennial reference book **The World Guide**, written by the Instituto del Tercer Mundo in Uruguay.

The co-operative is financially independent but aims to break even; any surpluses are reinvested so as to bring **New Internationalist** publications to as many people as possible.

'The **New Internationalist** magazine is independent, lively and properly provocative, helping keep abreast of important developments in parts of our globe that risk marginalization. Read it!' – *ARCHBISHOP DESMOND TUTU, Cape Town, South Africa.*